HALLOWEEN HIDE AND SEEK

HIDDEN PICTURE PUZZLES

BY

JILL KALZ

ILLUSTRATED BY

HECTOR BORLASCA

PICTURE WINDOW BOOKS

a capstone imprint

DESIGNER: LORI BYE
ART DIRECTOR: NATHAN GASSMAN
PRODUCTION SPECIALIST: DANIELLE CEMINSKY
THE ILLUSTRATIONS IN THIS BOOK WERE CREATED DIGITALLY.

PICTURE WINDOW BOOKS
1710 ROE CREST DRIVE
NORTH MANKATO, MN 56003
WWW.CAPSTONEPUB.COM

Library of Congress Cataloging-in-Publication Data
Kalz, Jill.
 Halloween hide and seek : hidden picture puzzles / by Jill Kalz ; illustrated by
Hector Borlasca.
   p. cm. — (Seek it out)
 Summary: "Illustrated scenes related to Halloween and monsters invite readers
to find a list of objects hidden within them"—Provided by publisher.
 ISBN 978-1-4048-7495-4 (library binding)
 ISBN 978-1-4048-7728-3 (paperback)
 ISBN 978-1-4048-7992-8 (ebook PDF)
 1. Picture puzzles—Juvenile literature. I. Borlasca, Hector, ill.
II. Title.
 GV1507.P47K345 2013
 793.73—dc23
                    2012007187

Printed in the United States of America
in Stevens Point, Wisconsin.
032012   006678WZF12

DIRECTIONS:

Look at the pictures and find the items on the lists. Not too tough, right? Not for a clever kid like you. But be warned: The first few puzzles are tricky. The next ones are even trickier. And the final puzzles are for the bravest seekers only. Good luck!

TABLE OF CONTENTS

4

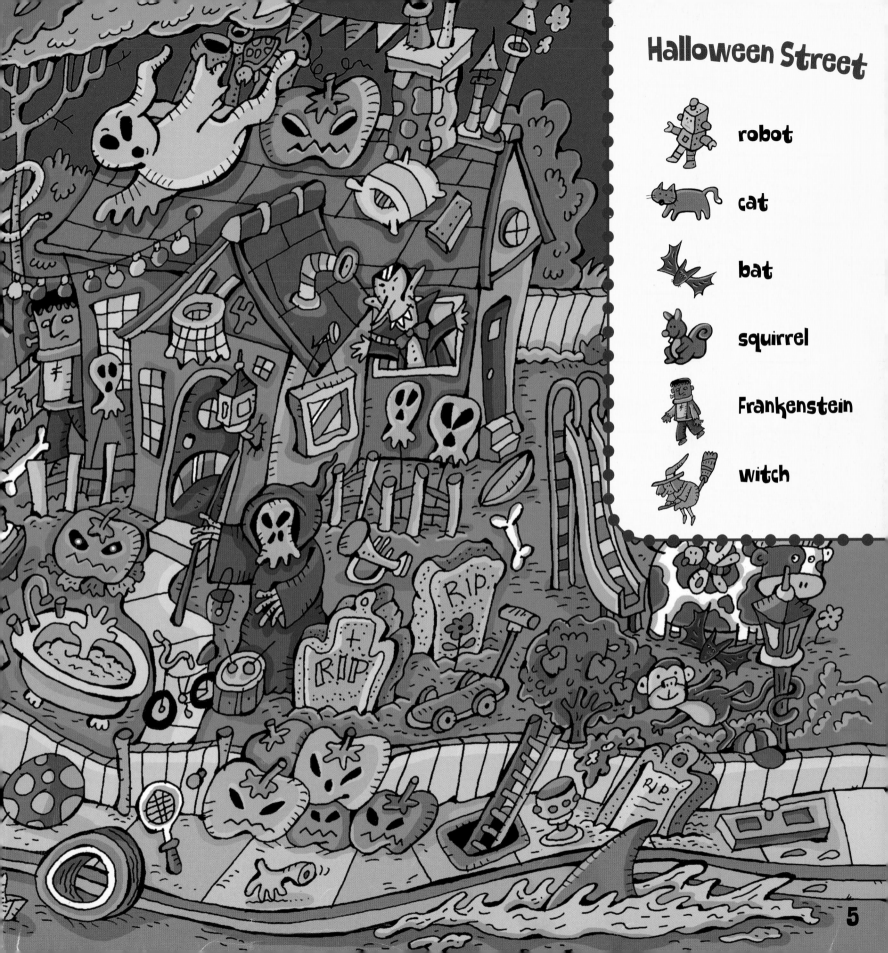

Halloween Street

- robot
- cat
- bat
- squirrel
- Frankenstein
- witch

5

Haunted Hash and Monster Mash

- cherries
- maple syrup
- take-out box
- pencil
- high chair
- rooster

BURGER

6

Spooky Lagoon

- treasure chest
- ship's wheel
- snorkel mask
- clown fish
- anchor
- sea horse

8

Gobs of Goodies

- toothbrush
- toothpaste
- pretzel
- hat
- pencil
- spider

Nightmares on Parade

- ♪ musical note
- crown
- pink sock
- sunglasses
- whistle
- lollipop

Monster Mansion

- scissors
- eyeglasses
- moon
- snake
- star
- broom
- tombstone
- owl
- lock and key

15

Too Ghoul for School

 pumpkin

 crayons

 spider

 top hat

 milk

 class pet

 globe

 jump rope

 pencil

18

Hide and Scream

- key
- dinosaur
- tennis ball
- green sock
- cookie
- party hat
- train
- orange crayon
- turtle

Pumpkin Picking

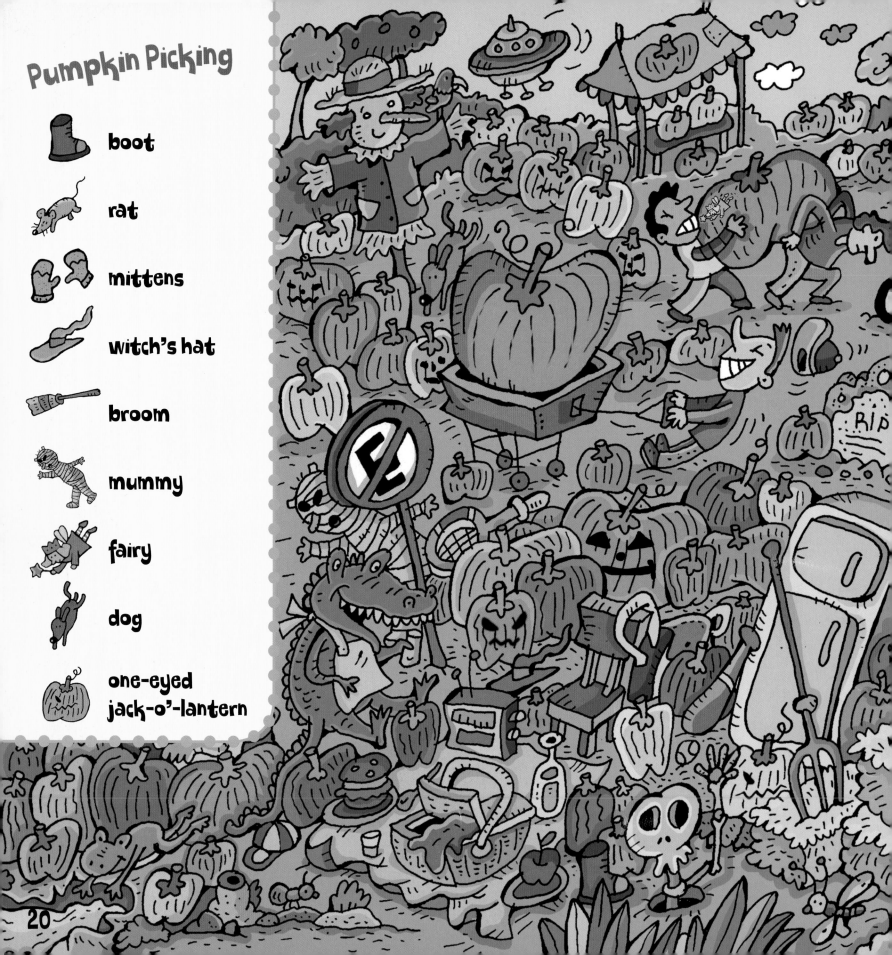

- boot
- rat
- mittens
- witch's hat
- broom
- mummy
- fairy
- dog
- one-eyed jack-o'-lantern

22

The Witching Hour

- candle
- magic potion
- piece of cake
- raven
- skull
- jack-o'-lantern
- spider
- pocket watch
- cat

23

Campfire Fright

 letters

 flashlight

 pumpkin

 canoe

 lantern

 guitar

 spiderweb

 heart

 baseball cap

 human spray

 tent

teddy bear

24

A Wizard's World

 shoe

 cookie jar

 postcard

 checkerboard

 snake

 unicorn

 dragon

 eyeball

 teakettle

 wooden spoon

 garlic

 skull

Alien Attack

 donut

 mushroom

 sunglasses

 hot chocolate

 cap

 woodpecker

 slingshot

 camera

 boot

 rabbit

 melted snowman

 football helmet

Tricks and Treats

- eye patch
- balloon animal
- magic wand
- broom
- guitar
- magnifying glass
- cowboy hat
- flippers
- fake ears
- watering can
- jack-o'-lantern
- glove

FOUND EVERYTHING?

Not quite! FLiP BacK anD see if you can finD these sneaky items.

31 number

school bus

blimp

peacock

windmill

can of worms

lamb

kangaroo

swan

trombone

Internet Sites

FactHound offers a safe, fun way to find Internet sites related to this book. All of the sites on FactHound have been researched by our staff.

Here's all you do:

Visit *www.facthound.com*

Type in this code: 9781404874954

look for all the books in the series:

CHRISTMAS CHAOS

HALLOWEEN HIDE AND SEEK

SCHOOL SHAKE-UP

ZOO HIDEOUT